After

efy,

So happy to connect with you here at IWWG! May your path be blessed with light, love + laughter

Judith

poems by

Judith Prest

Finishing Line Press
Georgetown, Kentucky

After

ACKNOWLEDGMENTS

"After" appeared in *Jump International Journal of Modern Poetry*.
"The Rape" appeared in *Recovering the Self :A Journal of Hope and Healing*
"Stillness Is like Water" appeared in the anthology *Moments of the Soul*, and
received 3rd Place in the Spirit First Poetry Contest
"Naming the Scar" appeared in the anthology *A Slant of Light: Contemporary
Women Writers of the Hudson Valley*

Publisher: Leah Maines
Editor: Christen Kincaid
Cover Art: Judith Prest
Author Photo: Ashley Holley
Cover Design: Leah Huete

Printed in the USA on acid-free paper.
Order online: www.finishinglinepress.com
also available on amazon.com

Author inquiries and mail orders:
Finishing Line Press
P. O. Box 1626
Georgetown, Kentucky 40324
U. S. A.

Table of Contents

After: A Journey to Myself
to every woman who has survived trauma
and discovered her own resilience

Poet's Prayer

Keep me from strangling
in the noose of my own
tangled thoughts,
give me the patience to free
each thread from the knot,
teach me to hold the
lines loosely.

Let me follow the pull
of the moon, trace
the veins of the oak leaf,
breathe in the sharp
scent of earth
after snow-thaw.

Let me remember the map
of my mother's face, how
I longed to know
the story of each line,
how I watched
death smooth and then
erase them all.

Allow me to keep
writing my own story
line by line
even in the dark.
Give me the grace
and the courage
to follow
each thread back
to the Source.

After

~ *fifty years later*

After the rape
the world tilted at
an odd angle
like a broken neck.

The sun still rose, I still
breathed, walked, spoke;
but there was an
impenetrable layer

between me
and the world
between me and myself.
No one could see it.

I was dimly aware that when
I tried to touch the surface of my life
it was like rubbing
a cheek numbed with Novocain.

My fingers can feel the skin
of my cheek
but my face does not
recognize the touch of my own hand.

The Rape
~ after thirty years

1.
a 747 crashed
into the sea of my life
left an oil slick on top
most of the carnage and damage
buried deep
deep below the surface

broken trust
broken dreams
black cold
smothering fear
so far from the light

hide hide
bury it deep
deny deny
make it go away
shame shame
"only you could
bring this on yourself"

2.
slowly
terror retreats
the tide of loathing
recedes into the depths
scar tissue forms
blocking light and life

never the same
never the same
no return, no safe places
ever again

3.
build a shell
body armor
blot it out
NUMB NUMB

build a false self
on top of the rubble
plant flowers
let it grow over

4.
years pass, life unfolds
finally
there is no moving forward
without a journey
to revisit the disaster scene

decades later
the way is clear
there are markers on the dark waves
beacons only I can see

time to strip down
dive deep into the dark cold
swim through silenced screaming
keep moving through terror
haul out debris
bring it finally
to shore

Why We Need Assertiveness Training

I am in eighth grade.
He is the music teacher.
He treats me like an adult.
Befriends me.
Says his wife doesn't understand him.
One day we end up
in the shadowy auditorium
behind the curtains and he
is kissing me. He has
bad breath.

I feel shame, confusion,
a guilty pride
that he has chosen me.

I shove all of it
into the iron box with the spiked lid
where I store unexplainable
exquisitely sharp
shards of experience.
The place I keep
what can't be spoken.

In the middle of my life
I find my voice,
pry open the box
am drenched
in a wave
of cleansing rage.

Unsafe

Because I felt unsafe
I pulled in all my colors
stifled my voice,
piled on pounds for armor,
stilled my body,
lived each day
frozen.

Because I felt unsafe
I worked hard to know
the invisible rules
so I could follow them
and not stand out.
Being who I was
felt wrong
and rude
as clowns at a funeral.

Because I felt unsafe
I laid low, took care
not to go
outside the lines.
The energy it took
to dampen anxiety's fire
could have powered
a small country
for a year.

Thunder's Name

This is the name of thunder:
boulders collide, magma and ash
burst skyward from the core,
earth splits wide
swallows
her own surface.

This is the name of thunder:
the utter stillness of a body
the moment after spirit leaves,
a booming silence launches
waves of sorrow outward
from the point of departure.

Thunder's name rumbles
when victims become survivors,
when slavery's chains melt,
when prison doors swing open.

Thunder's name reverberates
every time a woman names herself,
claims her birthright,
sends her power
into the world
blazing
like lightning bolts.

My Words Step into the Light

There were words
in me that stopped
my breath, cramped
my heart, stole my sleep.

There were words in me
buried for decades,
now they emerge blinking
into the light.

They stretch,
crack their knuckles,
flex their toes,
plant themselves
firmly on earth,
set my feet
to dancing.

"Choice"

Every conception
sets in motion
lifelong reverberations.
We do not forget.

I came late to this truth.
Once life starts, the world hums
at a different frequency.
Even those souls
who flicker briefly
make us mothers.

We do not forget.
We carry the memory
in our bones, in our hearts-
ghost limbs on the family tree.

We do not forget.

Motherhood Trilogy # 1
~ to my first one

Little spark of life
phantom child long gone,
I light a candle for you now.

I hold the pain
of your brief existence
deep in my body
cushioned against sharp edges
safe from cold wind.

Little spirit
long moved on,
the dues of your departure
paid in the currency
of tears and blood,
scalpels, gauze
and infertility.

Phantom child,
there is no measure
for this loss.
No accounting
can be made for
the time it took
for me to see you
at the borders of my life,
standing in shadow.

Motherhood Trilogy # 2

~ for Gloria, somewhere in Guadalajara

Sometimes, I feel my arms extended
through time and space
reaching for
your outstretched hands.

No doubt
what has brought me joy
has brought you sorrow.
Through your hard choices
I became a mother.

Two lives divided
by gulf and border
by miles of dry country
connected by sorrow and joy.

I dream our hands clasped
tan and brown
bridging canyons of pain
the raw power of our loss
and love
generating strong white light
to protect our son
and illuminate his path.

When I look into his eyes
when he smiles
when I greet him
in the morning
you are there,
a faint shape
at the edge of my vision
reminding me
that letting go
is an act of love.

Motherhood Trilogy # 3
~ for Jon

You stand midpoint in childhood,
and I remember
your baby cheeks,
our songs and stories,
your toddler delight
in pine cones and fireflies.

I see myself
weeping in the road
tears falling on the yellow line,
the kindergarten bus disappearing
around the bend,
removing you from
my circle of protection
transporting you into your own world.

Now you navigate the larger waters
of third grade
and I remember how you felt
in my arms that first time,
lighter than the cat.

I remember holding you
those first weeks
the wait finally over,
chanting, "Sweet One,
Sweet One, you are the one I waited for",
willing you to soak up
love and welcome
through every pore of your being.

I felt joy at your first steps,
then was stricken with the knowledge
that all steps after these would be
steps away from me
into your own life
if I do the job right.

I see you now
with wonder and gratitude:
your gentleness with animals
your concentration
as you draw a picture.
I wonder and worry
how you will negotiate
the territory ahead,
those years from 12 to 20
that nearly broke me
on their rocks.

I pray that my love
will be a beacon,
that my fear will not
obstruct your path,
that you will emerge
strong and sure,
capable and connected
a man of substance.

Witness

I am an ancient oak
anchored in stone.
I am oriole weaving her nest
with frayed string and dried grasses.
I am a new mother's heart
swollen with love.

I am a sliver of moonlight
through a cracked window.
I am the dream that sustains
the bruised woman.

I am a keeper of stories,
the silver strand
that will not break, the one
who holds the thread.

Metamorphic

Is it sick
or strange I wonder
to hold the
memory of pain
gently in my palm
turning it
over and over
a precious gem?

If I hold pain
in my hand
will it warm
to body temperature?
Will it respond
to the heartbeat
echoing so faintly
in the veins
of my palm?

Is it strange
to squeeze
the jewel of pain
in my fist, to crush
it with its own weight?
Is it crazed to wish
this lump of suffering
into a sparkling diamond,
a vehicle of light?

To Be a Woman

To be a woman you must learn
how to hold stories and pain,
how to recognize
the feel of high thread count
as you slip between the sheets.

To be a woman
you must learn
to balance a cranky toddler,
a looming deadline,
your checkbook,
with time to write,
and the simple act of breathing
and being
in the body you've inhabited
since birth.

To be a woman is to live in a body:
a body that has tides, seasons,
storms and droughts,
a body the world will hold
as the measure of your worth
and which you will struggle
to love and forgive.

To be a woman
is to assume the position
under the bright lights,
feet in cold stirrups,
all the most sacred places laid bare.

To be a woman is to know perhaps
the stir of new life in your belly
or the ache of breasts swollen
with milk that will never feed a child.

To be a woman
is to carry the weight of being a life bearer
or of bearing life
or the sorrow of knowing your branch
of the family tree will remain bare.

To be a woman is to know
you can love a child that did not grow in you,
enough to walk through fire for him
and to know somewhere in the world
a woman you will never meet
is praying you will raise him well.

To be a woman
is to know the dark ripping
as the rapist has his way,
and the steely glint
of your own resilience
emerging into sunlight
after decades underground.

To be a woman
is to find pockets of light
in the dark,
to know that even
as we wash the dead
and dress them,
we are planting seeds
for our own rebirth.

Stillness Is like Water

Stillness is like water
moving deep inside the earth
seeping slowly between rocks
trickling down
in the dark
a tide moving inward

Stillness is the space
between breath
inside heartbeats
the silence of the gathering wave
that never breaks

Stillness blankets me
cushions me against my own
sharp edges
wraps me in her protective shawl
keeps my tender heart
from ripping
on the thorns
of the world

Wildwoman, Closing in on 62, Takes Stock

Would you believe me if I told you I rode all the way up
the New Jersey Turnpike, into Manhattan, through the Village at 15
in the back of a '49 Dodge pick-up truck in the middle of the night?
Would you believe I drove for Teton Taxi,
I hitchhiked from Denver to Marble,
Would you believe I wanted to be a ballerina, a nurse, and then a wino bum
like the colorful characters in Tortilla Flat?

Come here. Look at me with a magnifying glass. Check out
the laugh lines, the frown lines, the grey hair, the scars—you can see
I did a lot of full tilt living, flying high—no sun screen, no seat belt, no net.
Don't you know I was lucky I lived to be 21?   Don't you know
I spent the first half of my life sticking out my tongue at danger, at death?

I threw away the proper white ankle socks I wore at 8 with my
Easter shoes, deep sixed my straight-laced grandma's
dire predictions of ruin,
traded in my training wheels for a fire-red convertible.

At midnight you could find me skinny dipping in the creek,
falling off my bar stool or
hollering at the moon in the middle of a railroad trestle.

Let me tell you something about trees:
they have been my solace, their roots
have held me to the earth more than once.
Let me tell you about the white pine
where I read and sang and dreamed so much of my solitary childhood.

Doors to me are scary opportunities—if I refuse to open a door
I will never know where it might have led. I mean,
what's the worst that can happen—
what might lurk behind a door that I can't handle?

Don't believe a word I just said.
Here's how it really is: for many years
I couldn't even see the doors,
never mind open them and walk through.   Now
I open the door to gratitude every time I remember.

It's not easy to forgive myself
—I'm not sure I have forgiven myself yet.

If you really want to know, I am most like a cracked porcelain bowl
repaired with gold, and every time one crack gets patched,
another opens, letting in some light.

Recovery Poem 1

I lost count
how many times I
fell down
fucked up
woke up
in the wrong
place

Can't remember
when
I knew
nobody
but me could
grab hold of
that space
between impulse
and action,
step off
the edge
of all I knew
and *fly*

Naming the Scar

some scars are visible
  red slash across the chest
  white ladder running up a cheek
  purple train tracks from collarbone
  to belly button mapping a
  chest cracked open to
  fix a broken heart

my scars run through every nerve
  panic and paralysis
  hair on the back of my neck
  goes up   breathing
  becomes difficult
  every muscle clenches

naming the scar
  alters everything
  to name it is to re-draw
  boundaries between
     before and after
     broken and whole
naming my scar
shatters the shell
I become
Survivor.

Demons

Embrace your demons
when they show up
in your house, your heart,
your dreams.
Do not resist.

Breathe from your belly.
Plant both feet
on the earth.
Look into their eyes.

Invite each one
to sit at your table
share your food.
Allow curiosity
to enter the room.

Ask where it hurts,
what will soothe its pain.
Keep breathing—remember
you are made of light.

Surrender.
When you place
your head between the jaws
of what terrifies you,
it will let go
and walk away.

Litany 1

~ *after Dianne diPrima*

"I have been a speck of sand under eternity's eyelid,
I have been the implacable force of a boulder, smashing all."

I have been salve for deep wounds.
I have been a song slipping into sleep.
I have smoothed ragged edges, erased footprints.
I have shaped and reshaped the border
between one world and the next.

I have fanned the fire of madness.
I have bathed sweaty skin, painting it
luminous in moonless dark.
I have gathered a gyre of trash in my far reaches;
I dare you to pass through it
and emerge alive.

Do you measure time by the tides?
Do you sing to receding waters?
Will the high-tide breakers carry you to shore?
I am the roar of tectonic plates ripping.
I am a silent burst of energy
crossing the void, the silence
that walks two steps behind chaos.

I have been your cool bed of solace.
I am soul swallower and life giver.
I am clear green light that can slice you in two.
I whirl and tumble you till your breath runs out.
I leave you awake to your own wisdom.

I am the boom of air colliding
in the wake of lightning.
I have been a wind stirred cauldron
and a bowl of tears.
I have been the vessel holding what land cannot.
I am an alchemist, empress of light.
I transform all I touch into gold.

This Time

This time I know leaving
will not rip me in two.
This time
I carry a piece of the fire.

I walk straight
balanced,
bearing wrapped fire.
Sacred embers glowing
deep inside fresh leaves,
traveling light.

This time a bright bridge
spans the gap:
it is no longer a flinty chasm
of rock shards
and dead wood.

This time I carry creation's fire
over the bridge.
My bundle is full but not cluttered.
What I need is near at hand.
I carry the fire
and it is enough.

What I mean is:
when I travel light,
the stars in my bundle
show me the way.

The Birds Showed Up

When my soul returned,
she rode in on a lightning bolt
drums beat,
thunder rumbled.

When my soul returned
birds were in the front row
   owl with her round golden eyes
   heron still as a blue feathered stick.

When my soul returned
the lake's surface
shivered,
the birch tree
curled her roots
around a stone.

When my soul returned
a flock of geese flew
across moon's silver face.
A great wind rose.
My ancestors arrived.

When my soul returned
I remembered who I am.
Gratitude carried me
to shore
and the birds
showed up.

Survivor
~ after St. Francis and the Sow, by Galway Kinnell

What does it take to reteach
a woman her worth
in the long aftermath?
How can she weave
something beautiful from the torn
threads of her life?

First she must turn
her face to the light, even
though this may magnify
her inner darkness,
even though it may be
skull splitting,
blinding,
searing as lightning.

It will take some time
for her to see colors again.
And, as with the temporary
deafness after gunshots,
she may not at first be able
to discern the notes
of her spirit song over
the ringing of her ears.

Bit by bit light will
penetrate,
warm and soothe her;
she will keep turning
towards the light.

Sometimes it takes the long
light of summer solstice
reflected from sparkling waters
to shatter the distorted mirror
she's been looking through.

27

To reteach a woman
her worth,
takes long silence
and deep rest.

Sometimes
she must allow
the light of joy,
the music of laughter
to carry her back
into her soul.

Judith **Prest** is poet, photographer, mixed media artist and creativity coach. Her poems have been published in *Writers Resist, Fredericksburg Literature and Art Review, Mad Poet's Review, Chronogram, Akros Review, The Muse~An International Journal of Poetry, Earth's Daughters, Up the River, Upstream* and in seven anthologies.

Judith spent 26 years as a school social worker prior to "retiring" in 2009. She now works part time providing Recovery Writing and Expressive Arts groups at New Choices Recovery Center in Schenectady. She also does creativity and healing retreats, poetry workshops and SoulCollage® workshops.

Judith was educated at The Evergreen State College in Olympia, Washington (BA) and at State University at Albany School of Social Welfare (MSW) and holds Creativity Coaching and Expressive Arts Certificates from New York Expressive Arts Studio. She also was trained as a SoulCollage® facilitator. Judith's art includes mixed media, collage and photography and has been exhibited in several venues in the Capital Region over the past five years. She is a member of The International Women's Writing Guild, Hudson Valley Writer's Guild and Foothills Arts Council, and is a Poetry Partner with Institute for Poetic Medicine.

Judith believes that creativity is our birthright as human beings. Poetry and art have been powerful forces for healing and growth in Judith's life. Her work now is to bring that out into the world, particularly to people who have not yet had the chance to discover this. She has led expressive arts and poetry workshops in retirement communities, prisons, treatment centers, school, libraries and at Spirit Wind Studio, her home base. Judith lives in Duanesburg, New York with her husband, Alan Krieger, and three cats. (*www. spiritwindstudio.net*).